Love and Marriage

Prayers, Poems and Scriptures

Regina Press
New York

First published in Great Britain in 1993 by
KEVIN MAYHEW LTD
Rattlesden
Bury St Edmunds
Suffolk IP30 OSZ

*Dedicated to the memory of our dear friend,
Harry Costello. We will miss you, and always treasure
the memories of our times together.*

GEORGE AND ROBERT

ISBN 088271 498 8

1996 The Regina Press

Printed in Belgium

CONTENTS

MARRIAGE PRAYER

Lord, help us to remember
when we first met
and the strong love
that grew between us;
to work that love
into practical things
so nothing can divide us.
We ask for words
both kind and loving,
and hearts always ready
to ask for forgiveness
as well as to forgive.
Dear Lord,
we put our marriage
into your hands.

To love and be loved
is the greatest joy on earth.

6

WINGS OF FAITH

Give us, Lord, a special faith,
unlimited and free,
a faith that isn't bound
by what we know or what we see.

A faith that trusts the sunshine
even when there is no light,
a faith that hears the morning song's
soft echo in the night.

A faith that somehow rises
past unhappiness or pain,
knowing that in every loss
your goodness will remain.

A faith that finds your steadfast love
sufficient for all things,
a faith that lifts the heart above
and gives the spirit wings.

LIFE'S LESSONS

After a while
you learn the difference
between holding a hand
and chaining a soul.
You learn that love isn't leaning,
but lending support.
You begin to accept your defeats
with the grace of an adult,
not the grief of a child.

You decide to build
your roads on today,
for tomorrow's ground
is too uncertain.
You help someone plant a garden
instead of waiting
for someone to bring you flowers.
You learn that God has given you
the strength to endure,
and that you really do have worth.

Faith, hope, love abide, these three;
but the greatest of these is love.

I Corinthians 13:13

9

DEEP IN MY HEART

Deep in my heart, my love will flower,
it is for you I long, love.
You fill my every waking hour,
you are my evening song, love.

I wish you all that's good and gold,
and pleasures ever-new, love;
but best by far, to have and hold,
my heart's desire is you, love.

My food and drink, my life indeed,
until my dying day, love;
my only joy, my every need,
come be my own, O stay, love.

MICHAEL FORSTER
BASED ON THE GERMAN OF PETER CORNELIUS

Be like minded, having the same love.

PHILIPPIANS 2:2

GOD HAS NOT PROMISED

God has not promised
sun without rain,
joy without sorrow,
peace without pain.
But God has promised
strength for the day,
rest for the labour,
light for the way,
grace for the trials,
help from above,
unfailing sympathy,
undying love.

May his love enfold you.
May his peace surround you.
May his light touch you.

GUIDE FOR A
LOVING HOME

May we treat one another
with respect, honesty and care.
May we share the little discoveries
and changes each day brings.
May we try always to be sensitive
to one another's joys, sorrows,
needs and changing moods,
and realise that being
a loving family means
sometimes not understanding
everyone all the time
but being there to love
and help them just the same.

Keep yourselves in the love of God.

JUDE 1

May God, who brought the two
of us together and joined us
as husband and wife,
affirm our love and make us one for ever,
blessing us with joy each day of our life.

May God,
who understands each need,
who listens to every prayer,
bless you and keep you
in his loving, tender care.

LOVE

Love is patient and kind;
it is not jealous or conceited or proud;
Love is not ill-mannered
or selfish or irritable;
Love does not keep a record of wrongs;
Love is not happy with evil
but is happy with the truth.
Love never gives up;
and its faith, hope and patience
never fail.

I CORINTHIANS 13:4-7

Lord, help us to remember
that nothing is going to happen today
which we cannot handle together with you.

LOVE IS GIVING

Love is giving, not taking,
mending, not breaking,
trusting, believing,
never deceiving,
patiently bearing
and faithfully sharing
each joy, every sorrow,
today and tomorrow.

Love is kind, understanding,
but never demanding.
Love is constant, prevailing,
its strength never failing.
A promise once spoken
for all time unbroken,
a lifetime together,
love's time is for ever.

22

Never Too Busy
To Care

Lord, make me so sensitive
to the needs of those around me
that I never fail to know
when they're hurting or afraid;
or when they're simply crying out
for someone's touch to ease their loneliness.
Let me love so much that my
first thought is of others
and my last thought is of me.

So God created humankind in his image,
in the image of God he created them;
male and female he created them.
God blessed them, and God said to them,
'Be fruitful and multiply,
and fill the earth and subdue it.'

Genesis 1:27-28

O Lord,
never let us think that
we can stand by ourselves
and not need you.

Trust the past
to the mercy of God,
the present to his love,
the future to his providence.

BLESS OUR HOME

Bless our home, Father,
that we cherish the bread
before there is none,
discover each other
before we leave,
and enjoy each other
for what we are,
while we have time.

Where you go, I will go;
Where you lodge, I will lodge;
your people shall be my people,
and your God my God.
Where you die, I will die,
and that is where I will be buried.
May the Lord do thus and so to me,
and more as well,
if even death parts me from you!

Ruth 1:16-18

Don't Quit

When things go wrong
as they sometimes will;
when the road you are trudging
seems all uphill;
when funds are low and debts are high
and you want to smile
but you have to sigh;
when care is pressing you down a bit,
rest, if you must,
but don't you quit.

Life is strange
with its twists and turns,
as every one of us sometimes learns,
and many a failure turns about
when they might have won,
had they stuck it out.

Don't give up
though the pace seems slow.
You may succeed with another blow.
Success is failure turned inside out

the silver tint of the cloud of doubt,
and you never can tell
how close you are;
it may be near when it seems so far.

So stick to the fight
when you're hardest hit.
It's when things seem worst
you must not quit.